J 789.1

Let's Make MUSIC

The Drum

and other percussion instruments

Rita Storey

W

FRANKLIN WATTS

LONDON • SYDNEY

First published in 2007 by
Franklin Watts
338 Euston Road
London NW1 3BH

Franklin Watts Australia
Level 17/207 Kent Street
Sydney NSW 2000

Art director: Jonathan Hair
Series designed and created for Franklin Watts by Painted Fish Ltd.
Designer: Rita Storey
Editor: Fiona Corbridge
Adviser: Helen MacGregor

Picture credits
Corbis/Jeremy Bembaron p. 23; istockphoto.com pp. 8, 10, 12, 14 (bottom), 15,
16, 17, 21 (top), 26, 28 (bottom); Odile Noel/Redferns p. 15, Toby Wales/Redferns
p. 25; Tudor Photography pp. 3, 4, 5, 6, 7, 9, 11, 13, 14 (top), 18, 19, 20, 21 (bottom
left and right), 23, 28 (top); Ulster Orchestra p. 24.

Cover images: Tudor Photography, Banbury

All photos posed by models.
Thanks to Husnen Ahmad, Serena Donnelly, Maddi Indun, George Stapleton,
Hannah Storey and Natasha Vinall

ISBN 978 0 7496 7583 7

A CIP catalogue record for this book is available from the British Library.

Dewey Classification: 786.8

Printed in China

Franklin Watts is a division of Hachette Children's Books,
an Hachette Livre UK company.

Contents

Words in **bold** are in the glossary.

The drum

A drum is a musical instrument made from a frame with a drum skin held inside it or stretched over it.

It is part of a family of instruments called **percussion**.

A drum.

Special brushes

Drum skin

Frame

Making a sound

To make a sound with a drum, tap or beat it with your hands, drumsticks, a **mallet** or special brushes.

You can play drums standing up, sitting down, or even as you march along.

This boy is playing a drum using drumsticks.

Listen!
Page 28 tells you about music played on percussion instruments that you can listen to.

Drumsticks

The sound

When you tap or beat the drum skin, it wobbles very fast. It is vibrating.

Vibrations

When the drum skin vibrates, it makes the air around it move as well. These **vibrations** in the air are called **sound waves**.

When you play a drum, some of the sound waves go down into the hollow body of the drum. This makes the sounds louder.

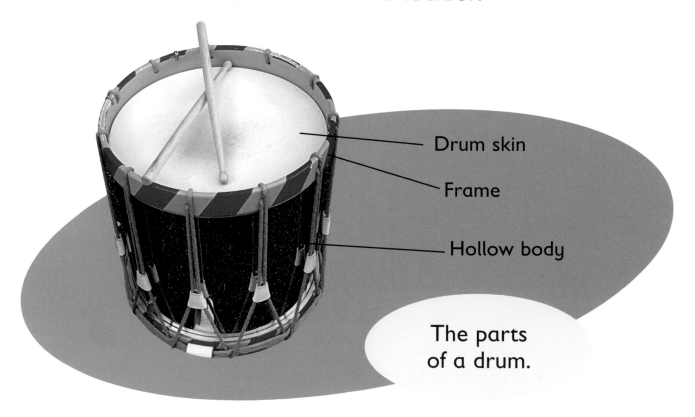

Drum skin

Frame

Hollow body

The parts of a drum.

Try this

Make a drum by stretching a piece of plastic over a bowl. Hold it in place with an elastic band. The plastic must be **taut**.

Using pencils as drumsticks, play the drum. Sound waves make the sound that you hear.

Put a few grains of rice on the drum and play it again. Can you see the rice moving as the drum skin vibrates?

High and low

Drums are made in different sizes and from different materials. Each one has a different overall sound.

Drum sounds and sizes

Some sounds are high and some are low. We say they have a high **pitch** or a low pitch.

A small drum has a high pitch. A large drum has a lower pitch.

This big drum has a very low pitch.

The way you hit a drum (hard or gently), and what you hit it with, also affect the sound it makes.

A drum kit is a set of drums and **cymbals** of different sizes. It has a foot pedal to work the hi-hat cymbals and another to make a **beater** hit the bass drum.

Cymbal

Tom-toms

Hi-hat cymbals

Snare drum

Floor tom

Playing a drum kit.

Bass drum

The beat

Drums are used to give a regular beat to a piece of music.

Playing the drums in a marching band.

Drums are popular in **marching bands** — the regular beat of the drum tells the members of the band when to take a step.

A **drummer** may play a different beat or rhythm with each hand and each foot.

Try this

Try tapping a regular beat (**1-2**; **1-2**) with a pencil on the table. Now tap a rhythm (e.g. **1-2**; **1-2-3**; **1-2**; **1-2-3**) with your other hand. Can you do both things together?

Music notes

Beat and rhythm

All music has a beat. This is a regular sound, rather like the ticking of a clock. The beat can be fast or slow. It is the heartbeat of a piece of music.

Rhythm is the pattern of sounds and silences within the beat of a piece of music.

Listen to some music. Can you hear the beat?

Playing a beat and a rhythm at the same time is very hard.

Shapes and sizes

Here are some more drums. They make different sounds because of their shape, the materials they are made of, and the way they are played.

Hourglass drum
There is a drum skin to play on each end of this drum.

Taiko
Japanese taiko drums are shaped like a barrel. They are played with drumsticks and make a very deep sound.

Timpani
These drums are shaped like bowls. They are very big and make a loud sound. They are played in an **orchestra**.

Bodhran
This Irish drum is open at the back. It is held in one hand and played very fast with a wooden stick.

Djembe
This drum comes from Africa. It is shaped like a drinking glass. The bottom of the drum rests on the ground.

Percussion

These shakers are unpitched percussion instruments.

Percussion instruments are a group of instruments that make sounds when you hit or tap them, scrape them or shake them.

They are often used to play the rhythm of a piece of music.

The sound they make depends on what they are made of, and the way that you play them.

16

Unpitched percussion

These are simple instruments. They may be made of materials such as wood, seed pods and gourds. The sounds they make do not have a fixed pitch – we say they are unpitched.

Pitched percussion

Some percussion instruments are tuned so that you can play musical notes. These are called pitched instruments.

The marimba is a pitched percussion instrument. Each wooden bar plays a different note. The tubes below make the notes louder.

Shake and rattle

The percussion instruments on this page are played by shaking them.

Maracas

Maracas have a hard outer shell made of leather, wood or plastic. There are dried seeds inside which make the sound when you shake them.

Maracas come from South America.

Make a simple shaker

Put a few pieces of dried pasta into a small plastic bottle, then put the lid on. Shake it and listen to the sound. Is the sound different if you put rice grains into the bottle instead?

All these instruments are shaken to make sounds.

Cabassa
This rattle is covered in beads. It comes from Brazil.

Sleigh bells
These bells are fixed to a wooden handle. They jingle when you shake them.

Castanets
These make a 'click-clack' sound. They come from Spain.

Beat it

Here are some percussion instruments that you play by tapping, beating or scraping them.

Tambourine

A tambourine is like a small, light drum that you hold in the air. You play it by tapping it with your other hand, or by shaking it. It has metal discs called jingles in the frame.

Playing a tambourine.

Jingles
These make a ringing sound when you tap or shake the tambourine.

Bongos

Bongos

These drums are joined together. You play them with your hands. One has a higher pitch than the other.

Tap and scrape

A triangle is triangular metal tube. You tap it with a metal stick. An agogo is made of wood. It is played by scraping a stick along its ridges.

Playing a triangle.

An agogo

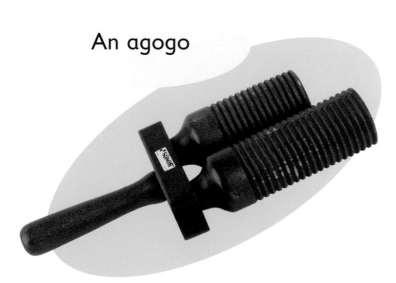

More percussion

You can use some strange things as percussion instruments.

Stomp

Stomp is a music and dance show. The performers use brooms, dustbin lids and kitchen **utensils** as percussion instruments.

Stomp performers using brooms to tap out rhythms.

A percussion band

Look for things that you think might make good percussion instruments.

Try to find things that will make different sounds. Ask your friends to do the same. Decide on a beat and a rhythm, then start playing percussion!

Dustbin lids and a cheese-grater played with a whisk make very different sounds.

23

The orchestra

Both pitched and unpitched percussion instruments are played in an orchestra.

A percussionist

A person who plays a percussion instrument is called a percussionist. The percussionist in an orchestra plays lots of different instruments.

Timpani

The pitch of these drums can be changed by pressing a foot pedal to make the drum skin tighter or looser.

Playing timpani.

This percussionist has lots of different instruments to play.

Unusual percussion

Percussion instruments can be used for special effects that add to the **atmosphere** of a piece of music. They can sound like thunder, sleigh bells or even frogs croaking.

Some composers include very unusual percussion instruments in their music. To make a sound like rain, the musician strings up a row of teacups and taps them.

Different styles

Percussion instruments can be used to play many different styles of music.

Steel pans

Steel oil drums can be turned into drums called pans. They are tuned to produce notes.

Steel drums are used to play Caribbean music.

This drummer is playing rock music.

Rock music

Rock music is another style of music. It is often loud and fast.

Listen!

Websites

Drums

Be a drummer and play a whole range of drums and cymbals by rolling the mouse or using the keypad on the virtual drum kit at:
http://www.kenbrashear.com

See Animal from *The Muppets* play a drum kit with the famous American drummer, Buddy Rich:
http://www.drummerworld.com/drummers/Animal.html

Watch videos of many exciting drum performances at:
http://www.drummerworld.com/drummervideo.html

Learn about Japanese taiko drums, listen to the music, see pictures of them and watch a thrilling video of a taiko performance at:
http://www.taiko.org/kidsweb/index.html

Percussion

Hear music that features several orchestral percussion instruments including cymbals, timpani, xylophone and bass drum at:
http://www.playmusic.org/percussion/index.html

Play interactive games to discover the world of different drums and percussion instruments. Some examples are the dholplayer (India), bata drums (Latin America) and gamelan (Indonesia). Go to:
http://www.bbc.co.uk/radio3/makingtracks/games.shtml

Watch the *Stomp* performers in action. You can see *Brooms*, a performance using sweeping brushes; *Pulse*, a movie of percussion rhythms from around the world; *Dolby*, played on dustbin lids; and the performers' appearance on *Sesame Street*. Go to:

http://www.stomp.co.uk/08_filmography.htm

CDs

Britten: *Young Person's Guide to the Orchestra.*

Bartok: *Sonata for Two Pianos and Percussion.*

Bernstein: *Symphonic Dances from West Side Story.*

James MacMillan: *Veni, Veni Emmanuel* (percussion concerto played by percussionist Colin Currie).

Steve Reich: *Drumming.*

Stomp: *Stomp Out Loud* (DVD of performances).

Madou Djembe: *African Drums.*

Palghat Raghu: *Impressions* (double-headed drum and tabla from India).

Gong Kebyar: *The Earth Meets the Sun* (gamelan music from Bali).

Glossary

Atmosphere Feeling or mood.

Beater Something used to strike an instrument.

Cymbal A piece of metal that produces a sharp, ringing sound when you hit it with a drumstick. Hi-hat cymbals are a pair of cymbals on a pole; when you press a foot pedal, they clash together.

Drummer A person who plays the drums.

Drum skin A piece of plastic or skin held inside a drum frame, or stretched tightly over it.

Frame The body of a drum. It holds the drum skin.

Mallet A type of hammer.

Marching band A group of musicians who play their instruments while they march along.

Orchestra A large group of performers playing various musical instruments.

Percussion A group of instruments that make sounds when you tap them, scrape them or shake them.

Pitch A high musical note or sound is said to have a high pitch. A low musical note or sound is said to have a low pitch.

Sound wave A wave that transmits sound through the air.

Symbol A shape used to represent something else.

Taut Stretched very tightly.

Utensil A tool, or a simple machine.

Vibrating; vibration Moving backwards and forwards, or up and down, quickly.

Index